Bacon

Bacon

RECIPES FOR CURING, SMOKING AND EATING

THERESA GILLIAM

PHOTOGRAPHS BY EJ ARMSTRONG

jacqui
small

First published in the UK and Australia in 2014 by:
Jacqui Small LLP
An imprint of Aurum Press
74–77 White Lion Street
London
N1 9PF

AUTHOR Theresa Gilliam

ART DIRECTION & PHOTOGRAPHY EJ Armstrong

COVER DESIGN Rachel Cross

INTERIOR DESIGN AND COMPOSITION Xiaonan Wang

RECIPES & FOOD STYLING Theresa Gilliam

A catalogue record for this book is available from the British Library.

ISBN 978-1-909342-78-1

Printed in China

10 9 8 7 6 5 4 3 2 1

CONTENTS

FOREWORD

Life is better with bacon.

It is a universal truth on par with the laws of gravity: bacon makes things better.

Throughout this volume we will expound on this theory with recipes like bacon baklava and rendered bacon fat in pastry cases. We will guide you through the adventure of curing and smoking your own bacon at home.

The glory of bacon is how it stimulates all of the senses. Salt and fat mingle with sweetness, smoke and crunch. It is a primal ingredient, a staple from our remembered palate. It recalls days of feasting and celebrations after months of toil. It deserves so much more than to stand guard over a plate of scrambled eggs.

BACON 101

The beauty of bacon is in its utter simplicity; a pork belly cured for 1 week, and then gently smoked with a flavourful wood for several hours. It is a sublime combination of salt, smoke and heat that carries with it a plethora of culinary wonders.

Bacon is our ode to bacon. Yet even bacon has a glossary of varieties available on the market.

GREEN BACON is cured but not smoked

UNCURED BACON is smoked but not cured

NITRATE-FREE BACON is often cured using the naturally occurring nitrates found in cabbage and celery rather than using chemically produced sodium nitrate

WET-CURED BACON is soaked in a brine before smoking

DRY-CURED BACON is rubbed with a dry salt mix before smoking

There is also variety in both the cut and flavour of bacon as well. Whether you are shopping at your local supermarket or visiting a butcher, you can find anything from slab bacon, thin-cut, thick-cut, maple-flavoured, peppered, applewood smoked, hickory smoked and more.

Use your favourite cut, flavour or brand and seek out the best bacon you can find. There are a few recipes where we may recommend using peppered bacon or a thin-cut bacon because we like the flavour or the texture it provides for that particular recipe, but the philosophy of *Bacon* is that cooking doesn't necessarily have to be an exact science, so we leave it up to you.

Now that you have purchased or smoked your own bacon (page 16) let's talk about how to cook it. Nearly every recipe in the book calls for a crispy cooked bacon. There are 3 schools of thought on cooking bacon; the conventional oven method, the microwave oven method and the hob method. Refer to the basic cooking instructions on page 12 when cooking bacon. It is important to remember that the bacon will continue to cook and crisp up after it is removed from the heat for another minute or two, no matter what cooking method you are using. For better results, bring bacon to room temperature before cooking, then place bacon in a room temperature frying pan or oven before turning on the heat. This will ensure that the bacon heats up slowly, maximizing the amount of fat rendered out of the bacon and will prevent scorching. Bacon can quickly go from perfectly crisp to charred and inedible. So whatever cooking method you choose, it's important to keep a close eye on it. It is also important to mention that cooking times may vary depending on the thickness, fat ratio and water content of the bacon you are using.

CONVENTIONAL OVEN METHOD:

Place a wire rack on a foil-lined, rimmed baking tray. Lay rashers of bacon flat on top of the rack without overlapping. Place the tray on the centre rack of a cold oven and turn the oven to 200°C (Gas 6). Cook the bacon for 20–25 minutes. There is no need to flip the bacon. Transfer the cooked bacon to kitchen paper.

MICROWAVE OVEN METHOD:

Lay 4–5 rashers of bacon in a single layer without overlapping in a microwave-safe dish, such as a glass baking dish. Cover with kitchen paper. Microwave on high for 4–5 minutes or 1 minute per rasher. Flip the bacon rashers and continue cooking in 1 minute increments until done to your liking. Transfer the cooked bacon to kitchen paper.

HOB METHOD:

Place the bacon in a single layer in a large frying pan or cast-iron pan. It is okay to overlap the rashers a little bit as they will shrink down with cooking. However, do not overcrowd the pan or you will steam the bacon rather than fry it. Place the pan over a medium heat and cook for about 4–5 minutes per side, turning often with a pair of tongs. Transfer the cooked bacon to kitchen paper.

PAR-COOKED BACON:

Place two layers of kitchen paper on a microwave-safe plate. Lay the desired amount of bacon in a single layer on top of the kitchen paper and cover with two additional sheets of kitchen paper. Microwave the bacon for 2–2½ minutes, or 30 seconds per rasher.

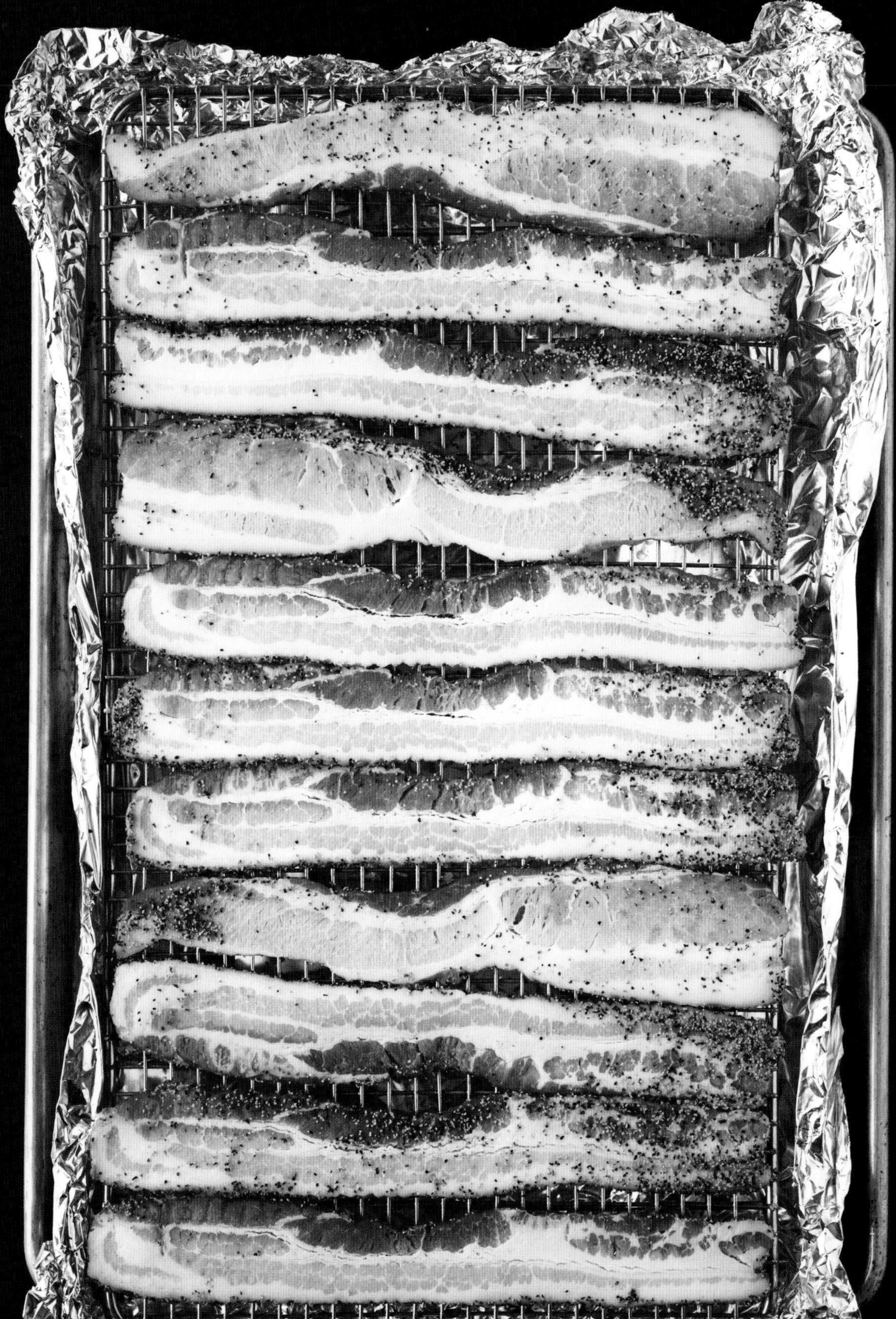

HOME-CURED AND SMOKED BACON

To truly immerse yourself in a lifestyle bordering on obsession, it is essential to venture into the world of home-cured and smoked bacon. Armed with a raw pork belly and a few speciality items you may find yourself never purchasing store-bought bacon again. With a little time, patience and the guidance provided in this chapter you will be a week away from enjoying your greatest culinary endeavour.

SOURCING INGREDIENTS:

Good bacon starts with a good cut of pork belly. Keep in mind that most supermarkets don't carry large slabs of pork belly like what is called for in the recipe. Most butchers should carry, or be able to special order, a 2.25kg pork belly with the skin on and the rib bones removed.

CREATING THE CURE:

To achieve the wonderful pink colour of traditional bacon and ensure that no harmful bacteria will grow during the curing process, it is important to use pink curing salt. This can be ordered online or purchased from speciality food shops. Do not confuse this with pink Himalayan sea salt; pink curing salt contains sodium nitrate. There are those who have concerns about nitrates and may choose to omit the curing salt from the recipe, but the bacon will cook up an unappealing grey colour and will likely be missing a certain savouriness that makes bacon so divine.

It is tempting to skip the resting step after the pork belly is removed from the cure but it is important for the meat to be dry and at room temperature before adding it to the smoker. If the meat is cold and wet it will not take the smoke well and all your time and hard work will be wasted.

SMOKING A PORK BELLY:

It is possible for most home cooks to smoke no matter what kind of barbecue they have. The key is working at a low temperature over indirect heat. There are a few tools available that will make life easier but are not essential.

For indirect cooking with gas barbecues: Fire up one side of the burners and leave the other side off. It is handy to have a stainless steel or cast-iron smokebox for your woodchips, which can be found at most DIY stores; however, a perforated pouch made out of heavy-duty aluminium foil will also work.

For indirect cooking with charcoal barbecues: Place a pile of burning charcoal off to one side of the barbecue and leave the other side bare. It is helpful to have a chimney charcoal starter. This will make replenishing dying coals much easier when the time comes and prevent the loss of precious heat and smoke while the barbecue is uncovered. Smokeboxes and aluminium foil pouches can be used on top of charcoal if desired but well-soaked woodchips can be thrown directly onto burning coals. Be careful not to add too much at once or you will extinguish the charcoal. Also, this method burns off the chips faster so they will need to be replenished more frequently.

For electric or charcoal smokers: Follow the manufacturer's recommendations.

This recipe can be prepared using the basic curing ingredients or feel free to experiment with 1 or 2 of the optional flavours listed below to create a unique variation.

Makes 1.8kg of bacon

2.25kg piece of pork belly
140g kosher salt
200g light brown sugar
1 tablespoon freshly ground
    black pepper
1 teaspoon pink curing salt
3 dried bay leaves, crushed
1.4–2.25kg hickory or
    applewood chips

Optional Flavour Variations
(choose up to 3 ingredients):
70–140g honey, warmed
70–140g maple syrup
70–140g treacle
10 sprigs fresh thyme
8 fresh sage leaves,
    roughly chopped
5 garlic cloves, crushed
2 tablespoons juniper berries,
    lightly crushed
1 tablespoon celery seeds
5–7 hot chillies, such as bird's-eye,
jalapeño or habanero

Trim the edges of the pork belly to make one long rectangular piece.

Combine the kosher salt, sugar, black pepper, curing salt, bay leaves and any optional flavours into a small mixing bowl.

Place the pork belly on a baking tray or in a large pan and rub generously on all sides with the salt mixture. Take a few minutes to vigorously massage the salt into the meat. Place the pork belly in a large ziptop bag or use a vacuum sealer if you have one. Discard any salt mixture that doesn't stick to the meat.

Refrigerate the pork belly for 7 days, turn once a day and give the bag a gentle massage. It will accumulate liquid and will begin to feel firm to the touch.

After 7 days remove the pork belly from the bag and discard the cure. Thoroughly rinse the pork belly under cold water and pat dry. Place on a rimmed baking tray or in a pan and refrigerate, uncovered, for at least 4 hours.

Remove from the fridge and leave to rest at room temperature for about 1 hour while you prepare the smoker.

Soak the wood chips in a bowl of cold water. Preheat the grill to 93°C using the indirect method explained in the chapter introduction. Smoke the pork belly for 2½–3 hours, or until the internal temperature reaches 66°C. Remove from the smoker and cool until it is safe to handle. Slice the skin off the pork belly, being careful not to remove too much fat. Cool completely.

The bacon will keep in the fridge for 1 week, or in the freezer for 3 months. To make slicing the bacon easier, place it in the freezer for 15 minutes before slicing. Cook the bacon using your favourite method (page 12).

CLARIFIED BACON FAT

Throughout *Bacon* you will note that some recipes call for Clarified Bacon Fat. We hope that you haven't been throwing away this precious commodity! Of course not. You are a true bacon afficionado. The culinary possibilities reach far beyond what is called for in this book. Use it to fry eggs, sauté greens, cook vegetables, toss into pastas, make southern-fried chicken or use it instead of shortening in baked goods. However, bacon fat does have more saturated fat, cholesterol, sodium and calories than butter, so use it with discretion.

Makes about 230g clarified bacon fat

230g fresh, rendered bacon fat
480ml cold water

Strain the rendered bacon fat through a fine-mesh sieve into a small saucepan. Add half the water and bring to the boil over a high heat. Reduce the heat to medium and gently boil for 1–2 minutes. Transfer to a heatproof container and add the remaining cold water. Refrigerate for at least 5 hours until the fat has solidified, or freeze for 2 hours. The mixture will separate into a layer of clarified fat, a very thin layer of fat mixed with impurities and a layer of water. Remove the solidified fat, shave off any impurities and discard the water. Place the clarified bacon fat in an airtight container and store in the fridge for up to 1 month, or in the freezer for up to 6 months.

TENDER AND FLAKY PASTRY CASE

The combination of butter and bacon fat creates the perfect texture everyone strives for in their pastry dough. This crust doesn't taste bacony so it can be used for both sweet and savoury recipes.

Makes 2 (23cm) pastry cases

400g plain flour
¾ teaspoon salt
170g unsalted butter, chilled and cut into 1.5cm cubes
4 tablespoons Clarified Bacon Fat (page 20), softened
1 teaspoon apple cider vinegar
3–5 tablespoons ice-cold water

In a food processor or in a large bowl using a pastry cutter, blend the flour and salt together until combined. Add the butter and fat and blend until the flour resembles coarse breadcrumbs. Stir in the vinegar. Add the water, 1 tablespoon at a time, until the dough comes together and holds its shape without crumbling. Form the dough into 2 discs, cover with cling film and refrigerate for 30 minutes. Use as needed. The pastry dough keeps for up to 2 days when refrigerated and up to 1 month when frozen.

To pre-bake the pastry case:

Preheat the oven to 180°C (Gas 4). Line a 23cm pie dish with pastry. Trim off the excess and decoratively crimp the edges. Pierce the base of pastry case all over with a fork. Refrigerate the pastry case for 30 minutes. Line the pastry with baking parchment and fill with baking beans or dried beans. Bake for 15–20 minutes. Carefully remove the baking beans and baking parchment and bake for an additional 10 minutes until the edges have started to brown. Leave to cool completely.

DAWN

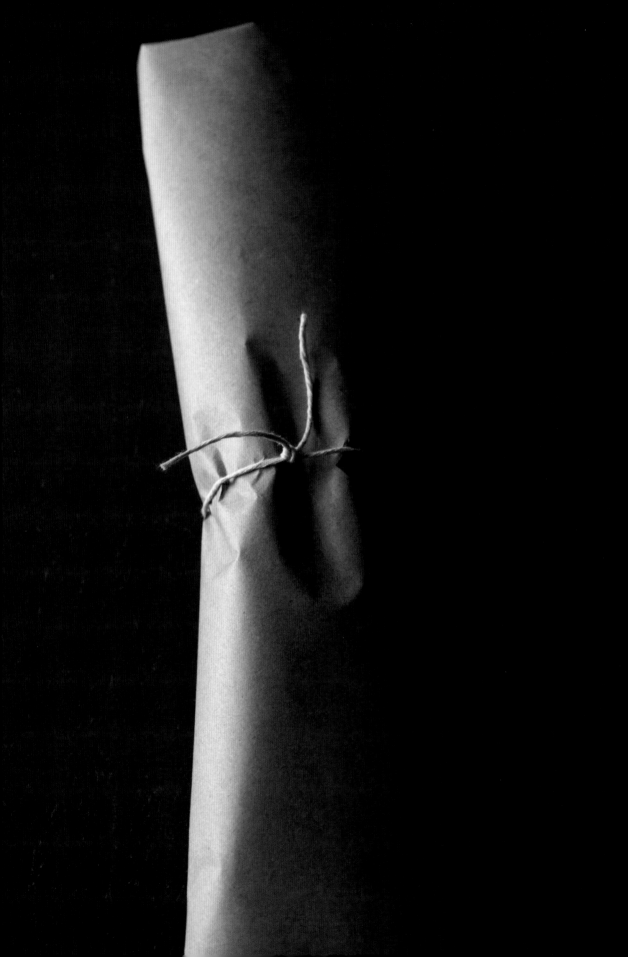

DAWN

BACON AND RED PEPPER STRATA

A strata is like a breakfast casserole. This version is marvellous for brunch or to feed a crowd for a weekend gathering. It can be completely assembled the night before so the rich egg custard soaks into the bread, then it takes less than an hour to bake. Leftovers are great warmed up in the oven.

Serves 6–8

6 rashers peppered bacon, cut into 2.5cm pieces
1 red pepper, deseeded and sliced
170g white mushrooms, sliced
2 garlic cloves, thinly sliced
6 large eggs
600ml full-fat milk
120ml double cream
20g thinly sliced chives
1 tablespoon freshly chopped oregano
1 tablespoon freshly chopped rosemary
1 tablespoon freshly chopped thyme
½ teaspoon salt
½ teaspoon freshly ground black pepper
1 loaf rustic French bread (500g), cut into 1.5cm thick slices
160g Fontina cheese, grated

Cook the bacon in a large frying pan over a medium heat until crisp, about 8 minutes. Transfer to kitchen paper, reserving the rendered bacon fat in the pan.

In the same pan, cook the red peppers, mushrooms and garlic over a medium-high heat until softened and beginning to brown, about 4 minutes. Stir in the cooked bacon and take off the heat.

Spray a deep 23 x 33cm baking dish with cooking spray and set aside.

In a large bowl, whisk together the eggs, milk, cream, herbs, salt and pepper.

Use half the ingredients to create the first layer. Arrange the bread slices on the bottom of the prepared baking dish, distribute the bacon, pepper and mushroom mixture over the bread and sprinkle with half the cheese. Pour half the egg mixture evenly over the first layer. Repeat with the remaining ingredients for the second layer, finishing with all of the remaining egg mixture. Cover and refrigerate for at least 1 hour, or overnight.

Preheat the oven to 180°C (Gas 4). Bake uncovered for 45–50 minutes, or until the egg is set and the top is beginning to brown and bubble.

Leave to stand 10 minutes before serving.

BACON CHEDDAR SCONES

These scones may be fluffy, but they are hardly what you would call delicate. They are sort of the 'work horse' of the scone world. Enjoy them alone, slathered in our Redeye Gravy (page 38) or create the ultimate breakfast sandwich. For variation, add chives, sliced spring onions or use grated Gruyère cheese in place of the Cheddar.

Makes 6 scones

270g plain flour
2 teaspoons baking powder
¼ teaspoon salt
100g Cheddar cheese, grated
4 rashers of cooked and crumbled
  bacon
360ml double cream

Preheat the oven to 220°C (Gas 7). Line a baking tray with baking parchment.

In a large bowl, whisk together the flour, baking powder and salt. Stir in the cheese and bacon until it is evenly distributed and coated with flour. Stir in the cream until the dough is just moistened, about 30 seconds. Do not overmix.

Turn the dough out onto a lightly floured surface and gently knead until it is just smooth, about 30 seconds. Pat the dough into a rectangle, 2.5cm thick. Cut the dough with a 7.5cm round cutter into circles, or use a knife to cut it into 7.5cm squares. Place the scones on the prepared baking tray, 5cm apart.

Bake for 15–18 minutes until golden brown.

*Over the top bacon lover's tip:

Before putting the scones in the oven, brush with a little melted Clarified Bacon Fat (page 20).

BACON REDEYE GRAVY

Redeye gravy was originally just a cup of coffee tossed into the frying pan to catch the flavourful bits leftover from frying-up ham. This is our bacon-take on the Southern staple. Espresso adds an extra kick. The gravy is best served warm with Bacon Cheddar Scones (page 35), but is also nice with fried chicken or pork chops.

Makes about 480ml

6 rashers of bacon, coarsely chopped
2 tablespoons plain flour
2 shots (60ml) espresso or
    120ml strong black coffee
240ml full-fat milk
60ml cream
¼ teaspoon salt
¼ teaspoon freshly ground
    black pepper

Cook the bacon in a large frying pan over a medium heat until crisp, about 8 minutes. Transfer to kitchen paper, reserving the rendered bacon fat in the pan.

Strain the rendered bacon fat through a fine-mesh sieve to remove any charred bits. Return 2 tablespoons of the strained bacon fat to the pan and warm over a medium heat. Whisk in the flour to form a roux. Cook the roux to a golden brown, stirring often, about 2 minutes.

In a separate bowl, combine the espresso, milk and cream together. Gradually add the milk mixture to the roux, whisking constantly. Add the salt, pepper and reserved bacon. Simmer, stirring often, until thickened, 3–5 minutes. Serve warm.

QUICHE LORRAINE

You may have guests begging you for your secrets to making this classic preparation. What will you tell them? Will you share the fact that you used two kinds of Swiss cheese? That it is double cream that makes the custard so rich and fluffy? We know that the bacon-fat-enriched pastry (page 27) is the real secret, but we will never tell!

Serves 6–8

1 pre-baked 23cm Tender and Flaky
   Pastry Case (page 27)
8 rashers of cooked and crumbled
   bacon
75g Gruyère cheese, grated
100g Jarlsberg cheese. grated
4 medium eggs
240ml milk
240ml double cream
1 teaspoon freshly chopped thyme
½ teaspoon freshly ground
   black pepper
¼ teaspoon salt

Preheat the oven to 190°C (Gas 5).

Fill the pastry case with bacon and grated cheese, tossing gently to combine. In a medium bowl, whisk together the eggs, milk, cream, thyme, pepper and salt. Pour the egg mixture over the filling.

Bake until the egg filling is puffed up and starting to lightly brown on the top, 20–25 minutes.

Cool for 10 minutes before serving.

MAPLE BACON TWISTS

We have to thank the geniuses at Voodoo Doughnuts in Portland, Oregon for inspiring these sweet dreams intertwined with a strip of thick, salty bacon, all drizzled with a glaze made with real maple syrup. It's almost too good to be true. You may need to clear your schedule for a month or two so you can make these EVERY weekend.

Makes 12 doughnuts

75ml warm water (43°C)
1⅛ teaspoons dry active yeast
  (½ packet)
50g sugar
1 large egg
3 tablespoons buttermilk
230g plain flour
¼ teaspoon ground cinnamon
¼ teaspoon freshly grated nutmeg
⅛ teaspoon salt
12 rashers of thick-cut, maple-
  flavoured bacon, par-cooked
  (page 12)
Groundnut or rapeseed oil,
  for frying
Maple Glaze (recipe opposite)

In the bowl of a stand mixer, combine the water, yeast and 1 tablespoon of the sugar. Leave to sit for 10 minutes to activate the yeast. Whisk in the remaining sugar, egg and buttermilk. Add the flour, cinnamon, nutmeg and salt. Knead the dough with the dough hook attachment until well combined, about 3 minutes. The dough will be very sticky.

Transfer the dough to a large bowl coated lightly with cooking spray. Cover and leave in a warm place to rise until doubled in size,

Transfer the dough to a floured surface and pat or roll it into a 2.5cm thick rectangle, about 20 x 30cm. Cut the dough into 12 (2.5 x 20cm) rectangular pieces with a pizza cutter or sharp knife.

Lay a rasher of bacon on top of each piece of dough and twist 2–3 times to form a spiral, pinching the ends to adhere the dough and bacon. Repeat with the remaining bacon and dough pieces. Cover and leave to rest for 30 minutes.

Preheat the oil in a deep fryer or large saucepan to 180°C.

Deep-fry the doughnuts, a few at a time, until the dough is fully cooked and the bacon is crisp, about 3 minutes. Transfer to a baking tray lined with kitchen paper.

Drizzle the doughnuts with Maple Glaze and leave the glaze to set before serving.

MAPLE GLAZE

210g icing sugar
70g maple syrup
2 tablespoons milk
1 teaspoon vanilla extract

Sift the icing sugar into a medium bowl and whisk in the maple syrup, milk and vanilla until smooth. Transfer to a piping bag or squeezie bottle or cover until ready to use.

GINGERBREAD BACON WAFFLES

These fluffy, yet substantial waffles have the flavour of a rich molasses cookie. The bacon adds an extra complexity and cuts the sweetness just the right amount.

Makes 10–12 waffles

400g plain flour
2 teaspoons baking powder
2 teaspoons ground cinnamon
2 teaspoons ground ginger
1½ teaspoons bicarbonate of soda
½ teaspoon salt
4 large eggs
130g dark brown sugar
360ml buttermilk
70g treacle
115g butter, melted
8 slices of Candied Bacon
   (page 154) chopped
Cooking spray or melted butter,
   for cooking

Preheat a waffle iron and oven to it's lowest setting.

In a large bowl, whisk together the flour, baking powder, cinnamon, ginger, bicarbonate of soda and salt. In a medium bowl, beat the eggs and brown sugar with a whisk until combined, then beat in the buttermilk, treacle and melted butter. Stir the wet ingredients into the dry ingredients until just combined. Do not overmix. Gently fold in the chopped Candied Bacon.

Coat the waffle iron liberally with cooking spray or melted butter and cook the waffles according to manufacturer's instructions.

Serve immediately or keep warm in the oven until ready to serve. Serve with your favourite toppings, such as, maple syrup and whipped cream.

*Over the top bacon lover's tip:

Brush the waffle iron with a little melted Clarified Bacon Fat (page 20) before cooking the waffles.

BACON RICOTTA CORN CAKES

These moist, flavourful pancakes are particularly delicious topped with a poached egg for breakfast or brunch. They are also fabulous served at dinner alongside ham or grilled salmon. They are as easy to make as any pancake, and are best served straight from the griddle for a perfect crisp exterior.

Makes 16 (10cm) cakes

140g frozen sweetcorn, thawed
2 large eggs
425g ricotta cheese
240ml full-fat milk
135g plain flour
150g polenta
50g sugar
2½ teaspoons baking powder
½ teaspoon bicarbonate of soda
½ teaspoon salt
6 rashers of cooked and crumbled bacon
Cooking spray or melted butter, for cooking

Pulse the sweetcorn in a food processor to a coarse purée. Add the eggs, ricotta and milk and pulse just until combined.

In a large bowl, whisk together the flour, polenta, sugar, baking powder, bicarbonate of soda and salt. Make a well in the centre of the dry ingredients and pour in the corn mixture. Stir to combine in just a few strokes. Fold in the cooked bacon.

Heat a griddle over a medium heat. Coat liberally with cooking spray or melted butter. Spoon a ladleful of the batter onto the hot griddle and cook until golden brown or crispy, about 2 minutes per side. Repeat with the remaining batter.

Serve the corn cakes immediately or keep warm in the oven (set to its lowest setting) until ready to serve. Top with poached eggs, if desired.

*Over the top bacon lover's tip:

Brush the griddle with a little melted Clarified Bacon Fat (page 20) before cooking the pancakes.

BACON-STUFFED FRENCH TOAST

Consider this for a decadent start to a lazy weekend or maybe a celebration feast after an active or productive morning. The orange adds a natural sweetness, so no syrup is necessary. Serve hot with a simple dusting of icing sugar and perhaps a scattering of fresh berries.

Serves 4

6 large eggs
120ml double cream
1 tablespoon grated orange zest
50g sugar
2 tablespoons orange juice
  (optional)
½ teaspoon vanilla extract
½ teaspoon ground cinnamon
½ teaspoon freshly grated nutmeg
¼ teaspoon salt
8 slices of brioche, 2cm thick
100g mascarpone cheese
8 rashers thin-cut bacon, cooked
  (page 12)
Cooking spray or melted butter,
  for cooking
Icing sugar and fresh berries
  (optional)

In a shallow dish, whisk together the eggs, cream, orange zest, sugar, orange juice (if using), vanilla, cinnamon, nutmeg and salt.

Spread each slice of brioche with 1 tablespoon mascarpone. Divide the bacon evenly among 4 slices of bread. Break off any extra bits of bacon to ensure that nothing hangs over the sides. This helps the bread slices to seal nicely. Brush the inside edges lightly with egg mixture and sandwich the bacon rashers with the remaining bread slices. Press gently to seal the edges.

Working 1 or 2 at a time, dip the sandwiches in the egg mixture. For best results, leave the sandwiches to soak for a moment or two, then flip and soak the other side.

Preheat a large non-stick frying pan or non-stick griddle pan over a medium-low heat. Spray liberally with cooking spray or brush with melted butter. Slowly cook the sandwiches until they are golden brown, about 5 minutes per side. Serve immediately or keep warm in a warm oven (set to its lowest setting) until ready to serve.

Dust with icing sugar and garnish with fresh berries.

*Over the top bacon lover's tip:

Brush the griddle with a little melted Clarified Bacon Fat (page 20) before cooking French toast.

BLOODY HELL
BLOODY MARY

There are multiple stories around about who created the original bacon Bloody Mary. The battles about who was first or what drink is best have been contentious and slightly sordid. This version is a total bacon bust that includes bacon vodka, Bacon Salt™ and a bacon twist garnish. It is so flavourful, you theoretically don't even need to add the booze – but in all honesty, the booze-less variety has yet to be tested. J&D's Bacon Salt is available online or at speciality food stores. If necessary, bacon-flavoured vodka, such as Bakon™ can be specially ordered online or at your local off-licence.

Serves 4

2 tablespoons Worcestershire
  sauce
2 tablespoons freshly squeezed
  lemon juice
1 teaspoon prepared horseradish
½ teaspoon hot sauce, such
  as Tabasco
¼ teaspoon celery seed
¼ teaspoon ground coriander
¼ teaspoon freshly ground
  black pepper
¼ teaspoon salt
480ml tomato juice
180ml bacon-flavoured vodka (or
  substitute plain vodka)
Lime wedges
2 tablespoons Bacon Salt
  (optional)
Bacon Twists, to garnish
  (recipe opposite)

In a measuring jug or pitcher, combine the Worcestershire sauce, lemon juice, horseradish, hot sauce, celery seed, coriander, pepper and salt. Add the tomato juice and vodka and stir well. Refrigerate until ready to serve.

Prepare four 240ml tall glasses by rubbing the rim with a lime wedge and dipping in the Bacon Salt. Fill each glass with plenty of ice and divide the Bloody Mary mixture evenly among the glasses. Garnish each glass with a bacon twist and a lime wedge and serve immediately.

BACON TWISTS

4 rashers of thin-cut bacon
4 disposable wooden chopsticks

Preheat the oven to 220°C (Gas 7).

Wrap a rasher of bacon around each chopstick in a spiral. Place the chopsticks on a rack over a foil-lined baking tray. Bake until the bacon is brown and crispy, 15–20 minutes. Cool completely before gently removing the chopstick from the bacon.

FATSO
CORNBREAD

Don't fight it! Embrace the decadence and slather each dense, moist and slightly spicy slice generously with Whipped Honey Butter.

Makes 1 (12.5 x 23cm) loaf or (23cm) round

2 tablespoons Clarified Bacon Fat (page 20)
225g yellow polenta
135g plain flour
2 teaspoons sugar
2 teaspoons baking powder
½ teaspoon bicarbonate of soda
½ teaspoon salt
2 large eggs
360ml buttermilk
2 tablespoons unsalted butter, melted
1 jalapeño chilli, deseeded and finely chopped
3 rashers of cooked and crumbled bacon
Whipped Honey Butter (recipe opposite)

Preheat the oven to 220°C (Gas 7). Place a 23cm cast-iron frying pan or a standard loaf tin in the oven with the Clarified Bacon Fat. Preheat while you assemble the cornbread, about 5 minutes.

In a large bowl, whisk together the polenta, flour, sugar, baking powder, bicarbonate of soda and salt. In a separate bowl, whisk together the eggs, buttermilk and melted butter.

Make a well in the centre of the dry ingredients. Pour the wet ingredients in, all at once. With a wooden spoon, gently stir the wet ingredients into the dry ingredients until well combined. Fold in the jalapeño chilli.

Remove the hot pan from the oven and brush the hot, melted fat evenly around the sides and bottom of the pan. Pour in the batter. Sprinkle the bacon on top. Bake until a cocktail stick inserted near the centre comes out clean, 25–30 minutes.

Serve warm with whipped butter, if desired.

WHIPPED HONEY BUTTER:

115g butter, at room temperature
3 tablespoons honey

Combine with an electric hand-held mixer and whip until light and fluffy, about 3 minutes.

BREAKFAST HAND PIES

This is an entire breakfast in one succulent little package of pastry. Use our bacon-fat-enriched Tender and Flaky Pastry Case (page 27) or your favourite commercial brand. Serve these straight from the oven with soured cream and salsa, or freeze them for a quick, midweek breakfast on-the-go.

Makes 6 (7.5 x 15cm) hand pies

3 rashers bacon, coarsely chopped
1 large potato, peeled and
   chopped into 1.5cm cubes
50g Cheddar cheese, grated
3 medium eggs
1 tablespoon full-fat milk
1 jalapeño chilli, deseeded
   and finely chopped
¼ teaspoon salt
¼ teaspoon freshly ground
   black pepper
1 recipe of Tender and Flaky
   Pastry Case (page 27) or
   1 pack (500g) shop-bought
   shortcrust pastry
Salsa, soured cream and fresh
   coriander, to serve (optional)

Preheat the oven to 230°C (Gas 8). Line a baking tray with baking parchment.

Cook the bacon in a large frying pan over a medium heat until crisp, about 8 minutes. Transfer to kitchen paper, reserving the rendered bacon fat in the pan.

In the same pan, add the potatoes and cook until they are golden brown and tender, stirring occasionally, about 10 minutes. Transfer the potatoes to a bowl with the reserved bacon and cheese. Toss to combine.

In a medium bowl, lightly beat the eggs with the milk. Stir in the jalapeño chilli, salt and pepper.

In the same pan over a medium-high heat, cook the egg mix to a loose scramble, about 2 minutes.

Add the cooked egg mix to the bacon, cheese and potatoes and stir gently to combine. Set aside and leave to cool while you prepare your pastry.

Roll out the pastry on a lightly floured surface and cut into six 15cm rounds. You may need to gather up the scraps and re-roll the dough to form enough rounds.

Divide the filling evenly among the dough rounds. Moisten the edges of the dough lightly with water. Fold the dough over the filling to create half-moon shapes and press the edges to seal. Use the tines of a fork or your fingers to crimp the edges. Cut 3 small slits on top of each hand pie to allow steam to escape.

Arrange the pies on the prepared baking tray and bake until golden brown and puffed, 15–20 minutes. Serve the hand pies hot with salsa, soured cream and chopped coriander, if desired.

FRIDAY'S FRITTATA

Frittatas are wonderfully adaptable. Slices of this family-sized omelette can be served hot or cold, for breakfast, lunch or dinner. Hemmingway put frittatas in between slabs of country-style bread for hearty sandwiches. This flavourful version might be best if it goes right in your mouth.

Serves 4–6

4 rashers of bacon, coarsely chopped
1 small onion, diced
1 garlic clove, finely chopped
360g baby spinach, washed and drained
1 tablespoon butter
6 large eggs
3 tablespoons milk
¼ teaspoon salt
¼ teaspoon freshly ground black pepper
2 tablespoons freshly chopped chives
20g Parmesan cheese, grated
Soured cream and hot sauce (optional)

Place an oven rack in the middle of the oven and preheat the grill.

Cook the bacon in a large frying pan over a medium heat until crisp, about 8 minutes. Transfer to kitchen paper, reserving the rendered bacon fat in the pan.

In the same pan, cook the onion and garlic until softened, 5 minutes. Transfer the onion mixture to a bowl. Cook the spinach in the pan until it is wilted and tender, about 2 minutes. Work in batches if necessary. Transfer the cooked spinach to a colander and squeeze out as much liquid as possible. Chop the spinach and add it to the onion and garlic mixture.

Melt the butter in a large, oven-proof frying over a medium-high heat. In a bowl, whisk the eggs, milk, salt and pepper together and pour into the pan. Gently stir in the spinach, onion, bacon and chopped chives. Cook until the eggs are almost set, about 5 minutes, occasionally lifting up the edges of the frittata and tilting the pan so the uncooked egg mixture flows underneath. Sprinkle the cheese over the top of the eggs and place the pan in the oven. Grill until the frittata is set and the cheese begins to brown, about 3 minutes.

Cut the frittata into wedges and serve immediately with soured cream and hot sauce alongside.

MIDDAY

MIDDAY

ALSATIAN TART

This French onion tart is a wonderful party dish that appeals to a diverse crowd. It is great cut into tiny bites to serve with chilled white wine before an elaborate meal, or as slices served with cold beer for the big game.

Makes 1 (25 x 30cm) tart

2 tablespoons olive oil
1 large onion, thinly sliced
½ teaspoon salt
½ teaspoon freshly ground
   black pepper
2 tablespoons white wine
1 sheet frozen puff pastry, thawed
125g crème fraîche
8 rashers of bacon, par-cooked
   (page 12) and chopped
20g Gruyère cheese, grated
20g Cheddar cheese, grated
Egg wash made with 1 egg yolk
   blended with 1 teaspoon of
   milk or water

Preheat the oven to 200°C (Gas 6). Line a baking tray with baking parchment.

Heat the olive oil in a large frying pan over a medium heat. Add the onions, salt and pepper and cook, stirring occasionally, until they are soft and golden brown, about 15 minutes. Add the wine and stir gently to dissolve any flavourful brown bits from the bottom of the pan. Simmer until the wine is evaporated, about 2 minutes. Remove the pan from the heat.

Roll out the puff pastry on a lightly floured surface into a 25 x 30cm rectangle. Transfer the dough to the prepared baking tray. Spread the crème fraîche evenly over the dough, leaving a 2.5cm space around the edge. Sprinkle evenly with the chopped bacon and onions. Top with the grated cheeses. Fold the exposed edges of the dough over the tart filling to form a 2.5cm border. Gently press the corners to help seal the edges into place. Brush the exposed crust with the prepared egg wash.

Bake the tart until the crust is golden brown and the bacon is crisp, 20–25 minutes. Cut into 6–8 slices and serve hot.

BACON AND APPLE GRILLED CHEESE PANINI

Get your sandwich press out of the back of the cupboard (or the garage) and prepare to fall in love with it all over again. Manchego cheese is a full-flavoured, firm Spanish cheese that melts marvellously. Use a good, aged Gouda for nutty complexity. But, let's face it, most any good cheese will make a divine sandwich when paired with crisp bacon and slices of tart apple. The Dijon adds a nice peppery tang. If you do not have a panini press, grill the sandwiches slowly on a lightly oiled griddle or frying pan, about 4 minutes per side.

Serves 4

1 loaf of foccacia or ciabatta bread,
   cut into 10-cm squares
4 teaspoons Dijon mustard
75g Manchego cheese, grated
120g Gouda cheese, grated
1 Granny Smith or similar tart,
   firm apple, thinly sliced
12 rashers of thick-cut bacon, cooked
   (page 12)

Slice the bread squares through the middle to make top and bottom slices. Spread 1 teaspoon Dijon mustard inside the top slices. Divide the cheeses, apple slices and bacon evenly among the bottom slices. Assemble the sandwiches and grill in a toasted sandwich maker or panini press according to the manufacturer's instructions until the bread is crisp and brown and the cheese is melted. Serve immediately.

FRISÉE SALAD

This is a variation on a classic French bistro salad. While the traditional version is topped with a warm poached egg, ours has baked slices of baguette slathered with goat's cheese. The dressing should be warm but not too hot, so it very lightly wilts the slightly prickly leaves of frisée. It's sometimes helpful to make a double batch of glazed pistachios. They tend to disappear.

Serves 4

2 tablespoons extra-virgin olive oil
8 (2.5cm thick) slices of baguette
125g chèvre (fresh goat's
    cheese), softened
4 rashers of bacon, coarsely
    chopped
60ml red wine vinegar
1 head of frisée, rinsed, cored
    and torn into bite-sized pieces
Freshly ground black pepper
Glazed Pistachios (recipe opposite)

Preheat the oven to 220°C
(Gas 7). Line a baking tray with
baking parchment.

Brush the olive oil evenly on
both sides of the baguette slices.
Spread the tops with 1 tablespoon
of goat's cheese. Bake on the
prepared baking tray until the
edges are golden brown and the
cheese begins to bubble, about
6 minutes. Keep warm while you
prepare the salad.

Cook the bacon in a large frying
pan over a medium heat until crisp,
about 8 minutes. Turn off the heat.
Add the vinegar, frisée and black
pepper to taste in the pan and
toss to coat. Serve the salad

immediately on individual plates
with 2 pieces of baguette and a
sprinkling of Glazed Pistachios.

GLAZED PISTACHIOS

1 tablespoon butter
70g raw pistachios, shelled
1 tablespoon sugar
1 tablespoon water

Melt the butter in a small frying
pan over a medium-high heat.
Add the pistachios. Sprinkle in the
sugar and toss with the pistachios
to coat, stirring constantly, about
2 minutes. When the sugar begins
to caramelize, add the water and
stir until the sugar dissolves and
coats the pistachios. Transfer the
nuts to a piece of foil or baking
parchment to cool.

POWER LUNCH
SPINACH SALAD

This is a well-balanced main course salad rich in protein and Omega-3 fatty acids. Serve it alongside grilled salmon and you can have your bacon and 'power foods' all at the same time!

Serves 4

175g baby spinach, rinsed
   and dried
12 rashers of cooked and crumbled
   bacon
225g mushrooms, thinly sliced
1 medium carrot, shaved into thin
   ribbons with a vegetable peeler
70g goat's cheese, crumbled
1 large avocado, peeled, stoned
   and diced
65g toasted walnuts, chopped
2 hard-boiled eggs,
   quartered lengthways
Walnut Dressing (recipe opposite)

Divide the spinach among 4 salad plates. Evenly distribute the bacon, mushrooms, carrots, goat's cheese and avocado among each serving. Top with walnuts and garnish with 2 pieces of egg. Drizzle the salads with Walnut Dressing and serve immediately.

WALNUT DRESSING

60ml champagne vinegar
1 tablespoon Dijon mustard
1 garlic clove, crushed
2 teaspoons finely chopped
   shallots
2 teaspoons chopped flat-leaf
   parsley
120ml walnut oil
Salt
Freshly ground black pepper

In a small bowl, combine the vinegar, mustard, garlic, shallot and parsley. Add the oil in a slow, steady stream, whisking constantly to emulsify. Do not add the oil too quickly or the dressing will separate. Season with salt and pepper to taste. Keep refrigerated until ready to use.

POTLUCK
POTATO SALAD

Inspired by German-style potato salads, the potatoes soak up the bacon flavour as it sits, so it is perfect to make ahead and take to a picnic or potluck event. Note, cooking the potatoes with the skins on prevents them from turning mushy when cubed.

Serves 8–10

900g new potatoes
8 rashers of cooked and crumbled
   bacon
35g spring onions, sliced
70g celery, thinly sliced
65g black olives, sliced (optional)
Sage Dressing (recipe opposite)

Scrub the potatoes and cut them in half. Cover the potato halves with cold water in a large pot. Bring to the boil. Cook until the potatoes are tender but not falling apart, about 20 minutes. Drain and cool until they are easy to handle. Peel and cut the potatoes into 3.5cm cubes.

Combine the cooked potatoes, bacon, spring onions, celery and olives (if using) in a large bowl and toss well with Sage Dressing until fully coated. Cover and chill for at least 1 hour, or overnight.

Serve chilled.

SAGE DRESSING

60ml white wine vinegar
1 teaspoon sugar
1 teaspoon salt
1 teaspoon freshly ground
   black pepper
½ teaspoon rubbed sage
120ml vegetable oil or
   light olive oil

In a small bowl, whisk together the vinegar, sugar, salt, pepper and sage. Add the oil in a slow, steady stream, whisking constantly. Refrigerate until ready to use.

*Over the top bacon lover's tip:

Toss the cooked, cubed potatoes in 1–2 tablespoons Clarified Bacon Fat (page 20) before adding the remaining ingredients.

BACON BLT SANDWICH

Real bacon lovers don't settle for a simple BLT. This is our, over-the-top version, with freshly made Bacon Mayonnaise on thick rashers of crispy, smoked bacon with avocado, rocket leaves and juicy slices of sweet heritage tomato. Bacon mayonnaise is available commercially, but nothing compares to this version made with real bacon fat. We like a locally made rustic multi-grain bread, but you can substitute your favourite.

Makes 4 sandwiches

50g Bacon Mayonnaise,
   about 3–4 tablespoons
   (recipe opposite)
8 slices of fresh, crusty multi-grain
   bread, toasted
8 slices heritage tomato
   (or any ripe tomato)
1 avocado, peeled, stoned
   and sliced
140g rocket, loosely packed
12 rashers of thick-cut bacon,
   cooked (page 12)

Spread the Bacon Mayonnaise liberally on the toast slices. Divide the tomato slices, avocado slices and rocket evenly among 4 slices of bread. Top with the bacon and the remaining pieces of toast. Serve immediately.

BACON MAYONNAISE

2 egg yolks
1 teaspoon Dijon mustard
1 teaspoon freshly squeezed
   lemon juice
125g Clarified Bacon Fat, melted,
   but not hot (page 20)
60ml vegetable oil or light
   olive oil
¾ teaspoon salt
Freshly ground white pepper

Combine the egg yolks, mustard and lemon juice in the bowl of a food processor, blender or stand mixer. Combine the bacon fat and oil in a liquid measuring jug. With the machine running, gradually add the oil and fat, a few drops at a time, to the egg mixture. Gradually increase to a thin stream to form a fully emulsified mayonnaise. Season to taste with salt and pepper. Refrigerate until ready to use. Because of the bacon fat, the mayonnaise may harden more than usual when it is chilled. It can still be spread, or you can leave it at room temperature for 30 minutes to soften.

DECONSTRUCTED BLT

Like gazpacho, this soup is best when it is made with the freshest, most flavourful summer produce. All of the components of a classic BLT are in here, but the presentation is all new. The bread is part of the broth, the lettuce forms the cup and the soup is garnished with 'cookies' – delicate discs of crisp bacon made from pressed and moulded slivers of sliced bacon.

Serves 6

360ml tomato juice
100g French bread, crust removed
  and cut into 2.5cm cubes
12 medium-sized tomatoes
  peeled, deseeded and chopped
1 cucumber, peeled, deseeded
  and chopped
3 garlic cloves, chopped
65g red pepper, chopped
65g red onion, chopped
10g fresh coriander, chopped
2 tablespoons freshly squeezed
  lime juice
2 teaspoons salt
2 teaspoons smoked paprika
1 teaspoon ground cumin
¼ teaspoon freshly ground
  black pepper
240ml extra-virgin olive oil
6 flat lettuce leaves,
  washed and dried
Additional diced cucumber,
  to garnish
6 (7.5cm) Bacon 'Cookies'
  (recipe opposite)

In a small bowl, combine the tomato juice and bread cubes and leave to soak until the bread is very soft, about 30 minutes.

Transfer the mixture to a blender and purée until smooth. Add the tomatoes, cucumber, garlic, red pepper, onion, coriander, lime juice, salt, paprika, cumin and pepper. Blend to a very smooth purée. You may need to work in batches. With the mixer running on high speed, add the oil slowly, in a steady stream. Cover and refrigerate the gazpacho until it is well chilled, at least 1 hour.

Place a lettuce leaf in the centre of 6 bowls. Ladle the chilled gazpacho over lettuce cups into the bowls, sprinkle with diced cucumber and garnish with a Bacon 'Cookie'. Serve immediately.

BACON 'COOKIES'

Makes 6

6 rashers of bacon, sliced into
  3mm slivers

Preheat the oven to 200°C (Gas 6). Line a baking tray with baking parchment. Make 'cookies' by packing 1 rasher of slivered bacon, about 2 tablespoons, into a 7.5cm ring or biscuit cutter. Lift the ring or cutter off, leaving a round of compressed bacon slivers. Repeat with the remaining bacon. Bake until brown and crispy, about 15 minutes. Carefully remove the bacon 'cookies from the tray with a spatula and transfer to kitchen paper to cool.

BROS, BEERS AND BRATS

Are you one of those people with a brother who considers brats and beer to be his 'special' recipe? Maybe you are that brother? Even if you are an only child, this bacon-enriched, sauerkraut-simmered variation of the Midwestern classic is how good brats deserve to be done.

Serves 6

8 rashers of bacon, chopped into
   5cm pieces
1 large onion, thinly sliced
1 bottle of lager-style beer
   (340ml)
480g sauerkraut, drained
2 tablespoons ketchup
1 teaspoon caraway seeds
1 teaspoon fennel seeds
1 teaspoon cracked black
   peppercorns
2 bay leaves
6 bratwurst sausages
Rye bread or sub rolls
Stoneground or Dijon mustard

Heat a large, deep sauté pan or casserole over a medium heat. Cook the bacon until it is brown, but not completely crisp, about 5 minutes. Add the onion and cook until soft and golden, about 7 minutes. Deglaze the pan with half the beer, scraping gently to dissolve any brown bits. Stir in the sauerkraut, ketchup, caraway seeds, fennel seeds, peppercorns and remaining beer.

Add the bay leaves. Bring the sauerkraut to the boil, then reduce the heat to medium-low.

Pierce each bratwurst on both sides with the tip of a knife. Nestle the sausages into the sauerkraut. Cover the pan and simmer for 20–25 minutes, turning the sausages and stirring the sauerkraut occasionally. At this point the sausages can be served as is, or if you prefer a crispier skin for your bratwurst continue as follows.

Position a rack in the centre of the oven and preheat the grill.

Lift the cooked sausages from the sauerkraut and arrange them on a lightly-greased, foil-lined baking tray. Grill until the edges of the sausages begin to brown, about 3–5 minutes per side.

Serve the bratwurst with sauerkraut on rye bread or in sub rolls slathered with mustard.

BACON
BUTTERNUT
SQUASH SOUP

This is a velvety, comforting soup garnished with bacon, crispy fried sage leaves and roasted, salted pumpkin seeds. It is perfect for autumn or winter. Serve it in tiny bowls as a first course, or in bigger portions as a main course.

Serves 4–6

6 rashers of bacon, coarsely chopped
3 carrots, chopped
2 shallots, finely chopped
2 garlic cloves, crushed
1 teaspoon salt
½ teaspoon freshly ground black pepper
1 tablespoon chopped fresh sage
2 teaspoons chopped fresh thyme
1 bay leaf
680g (2.5cm cubes) fresh or frozen butternut squash
1 litre chicken or vegetable stock
1 teaspoon apple cider vinegar
¼ teaspoon grated nutmeg
35g roasted, salted pumpkin seeds
Fried Sage Leaves (recipe opposite)

Cook the bacon in a large saucepan over a medium heat until almost crisp, about 6 minutes. Transfer to kitchen paper, reserving the rendered bacon fat in the pan.

Cook the carrots, shallots and garlic in the reserved bacon fat until soft and golden, about 5 minutes. Stir in the salt and pepper. Add the chopped herbs, bay leaf, cubed squash, stock and half the cooked bacon to the soup pan. Bring the soup to the boil, then reduce the heat to medium-low and simmer, stirring occasionally, until the squash is tender, 20–25 minutes. Remove and discard the bay leaf.

Blend the soup to a smooth purée with a hand-held electric blender or in batches in a traditional blender. Season with vinegar and nutmeg. Keep the soup warm until it is ready to serve.

Ladle the soup into warm bowls and garnish with the reserved bacon, roasted pumpkin seeds and the Fried Sage Leaves.

FRIED SAGE LEAVES

Vegetable oil, for deep-frying
10–12 fresh sage leaves

Heat the oil in a saucepan to 180°C. Deep-fry the sage leaves until they are crisp, about 10 seconds. Transfer to kitchen paper.

BLT MAC AND CHEESE

Bacon and melted cheese is a magical pairing, but many bacon mac and cheese recipes seem intensely salty or cloying. BLT mac and cheese... now that's a whole different story! Tomatoes and fresh basil brighten up the dish for a much better balance. The dish is still very rich, which is why we include the 'L' as a simple, crisp salad served alongside. To keep the pasta from absorbing too much liquid, we assemble the casserole at the last minute and brown it in a hot oven.

Serves 6

225g cellantani or similar
 curly pasta
6 rashers of bacon, coarsely
 chopped
2 leeks, halved lengthways
 and sliced, white and light
 green parts only
2 garlic cloves, chopped
¼ teaspoon chilli flakes
60ml single cream
60ml full-fat milk
60ml tomato sauce
225g mascarpone cheese
80g Parmesan cheese, grated
Salt
Freshly ground black pepper
170g cherry tomatoes, halved
35g basil leaves, chopped
20g dry breadcrumbs
400–500g rocket or baby
 spinach, washed and dried
Sage Dressing (page 75) made
 with basil, or substitute your
 favourite vinaigrette

Preheat the oven to 230°C (Gas 8). Lightly grease a deep (23 x 33cm) casserole or baking dish.

Bring a large saucepan of salted water to the boil. Add the pasta and cook, according to packet instructions, until al dente. Drain.

Cook the bacon in a large frying pan over a medium heat until just starting to crisp, about 6 minutes. Add the leeks and cook until they are softened, 2–3 minutes. Add the garlic and chilli flakes and cook for 1 minute more. Stir in the cream, milk and tomato sauce until well combined. Add the mascarpone cheese and simmer, stirring constantly, until it is melted. Remove the pan from the heat, add three-quarters of the Parmesan cheese and season to taste with salt and pepper.

Combine the sauce, cooked pasta, cherry tomatoes and basil and gently toss to coat. Transfer to the prepared casserole or baking dish and sprinkle with the breadcrumbs and remaining Parmesan cheese. Bake until bubbling at the edges and browned on top, about 15 minutes.

In a large bowl, toss the rocket or spinach with vinaigrette. Serve the greens alongside warm portions of pasta.

STEAMED MUSSELS WITH TOMATO AND FENNEL

Cooking mussels with tomatoes and fennel in a light bacon broth creates a dish reminiscent of sea breezes. You'll need a whole loaf of crusty bread to sop up all the precious broth.

Serves 4

900g fresh mussels
6 rashers of bacon, coarsely chopped
1 large shallot, finely chopped
4 garlic cloves, crushed
1 fennel bulb, sliced
480ml dry white wine, such as a
    Sauvignon Blanc
115g butter, melted
1 (400g) tin of plum tomatoes
20g basil leaves, chopped
3 tablespoons chopped flat-leaf parsley
Fresh, crusty bread or baguette

Scrub and de-beard the mussels.

Cook the bacon in a large saucepan over a medium heat until it is almost crisp, about 6 minutes. Add the shallots, garlic and fennel and cook for 1 minute. Add the mussels to the pan along with the wine and butter. Lightly crush the tomatoes by hand and add them to the pan with the juices. Cover and cook, stirring occasionally, until all of the mussels have opened, about 7–10 minutes. Remove from the heat and stir in the basil and parsley.

Ladle the mussels and broth into bowls and serve hot with plenty of bread for dipping in the broth.

GRAPE AND GORGONZOLA PIZZETTAS

Individual 'pizzettas' like these
are the perfect size for a light
lunch, starter, a cocktail nosh
or a late-night snack. Use your
favourite pizza dough recipe or
any good-quality shop-bought
pizza dough.

Makes 4 (15cm) individual pizzas

1 packet (450g) prepared
   pizza dough
500g red seedless grapes,
   rinsed and stemmed
1 large red onion, thinly sliced
60ml olive oil
¾ teaspoon salt
200g ricotta cheese
1 tablespoon Italian seasoning
1 teaspoon chopped garlic
¼ teaspoon freshly ground
   black pepper
225g Gorgonzola cheese, crumbled
8 rashers of thick-cut, peppered
   bacon, par-cooked (page 12)
Fresh herbs, such as thyme,
   pregano or marjoram, to garnish

If the pizza dough is cold, leave it
to sit at room temperature while
you prepare the toppings.

If you have a pizza stone, put it in
the cold oven. If you do not have
a pizza stone, the pizzettas can be
baked on a baking tray. Preheat
the oven to 230°C (Gas 8).

Toss the grapes and onions with
about 3 tablespoons of the olive
oil and ½ teaspoon of the salt.
Spread them in a single layer on a
baking tray. Roast until the grapes
are wrinkled and the onions are
soft, about 25 minutes.

In a medium bowl, mix together
the ricotta, Italian seasoning,
garlic, pepper and the remaining
olive oil and salt.

Divide the pizza dough into four
equal pieces.

On a lightly floured surface or
floured pizza peel, roll out the
dough pieces into 15cm rounds.
Spread a quarter of the ricotta
mixture onto each pizza, leaving
1.5cm of space around the edges.
Cover each pizza evenly with
the grape and onion mixture and
crumbled Gorgonzola cheese.
Break 2 rashers of bacon onto
each pizza. Bake the pizzettas
on the preheated pizza stone
or on lightly oiled baking trays
until the crust is golden brown,
10–12 minutes.

Garnish with fresh herbs and
serve hot.

DUSK

DUSK

TERIYAKI SALMON SKEWERS WITH BACON AND PINEAPPLE

One skewer has all the flavours and textures you can imagine – salty, sweet, savoury, tangy, silky, crisp and fresh. Once you learn how simple it is to throw together a perfect teriyaki sauce, you will never go back to the commercial bottles. Mirin is a very mild, sweet Japanese rice wine. Use only top-quality salmon for the best results. Weaving the bacon and assorted ingredients together on the skewer looks nice, but it also secures the bacon on the skewer more solidly and helps to distribute the flavour and fat evenly.

Makes 20 skewers

120ml soy sauce
2 tablespoons mirin
2 tablespoons rice wine vinegar
2 tablespoons light brown sugar
1 tablespoon grated fresh ginger
680g salmon fillet, skin and
   pin bones removed, cut into
   2.5cm cubes
Salt
10 rashers of thick-cut bacon,
   cut in half crossways,
   par-cooked (page 12)
1 fresh pineapple, peeled,
   cored and cut into 5cm cubes
Sesame seeds, to garnish

20 bamboo skewers

Combine the soy sauce, mirin, vinegar, brown sugar and ginger in a small saucepan. Bring to the boil over a high heat, then simmer over a medium-low heat until the sauce has reduced by half, about 10 minutes. Pour half of the sauce into a small serving dish.

Preheat the oven to 200°C (Gas 6).

Line a baking tray with foil and place a wire rack on top. Season the salmon cubes well with salt. Weave a slice of bacon onto each bamboo skewer, followed by one piece of pineapple and finishing with a cube of salmon. Place the skewer on the rack and repeat with the remaining ingredients and skewers.

Brush each skewer with the teriyaki sauce. Bake the glazed skewers until the bacon is crisp and the salmon is just cooked through, 5–7 minutes.

Serve warm with the reserved bowl of teriyaki sauce and toasted sesame seeds (optional) alongside.

BACON-WRAPPED SCALLOPS WITH PAPAYA PINEAPPLE GLAZE

Bacon-wrapped scallops are wildly popular, and with good reason. This version uses good-quality, plump sea scallops and adds a hint of the tropics with reduced papaya nectar and pineapple juice. Served on a bed of wild rice, this is a wonderfully elegant dish for entertaining. Papaya nectar is available at gourmet supermarkets.

Serves 4

12 sea scallops
240ml papaya nectar or juice
120ml pineapple juice
2 tablespoons freshly squeezed
  lime juice
1 teaspoon grated ginger
Salt
Freshly ground black pepper
12 rashers of thin-cut bacon,
  par-cooked (page 12)
4 tablespoons butter

Rinse and dry the scallops. Remove and discard the small, tough muscle from the sides of the scallops if they haven't already been removed. Refrigerate until ready to use.

Combine the papaya nectar, pineapple juice, lime juice and ginger in a saucepan. Bring to the boil on a high heat and then reduce the heat to medium. Simmer until it is reduced to a syrupy glaze, about 20 minutes.

Season the scallops with salt and pepper. Wrap one piece of bacon around each scallop, securing overlapping edges with cocktail sticks. Melt the butter in a large frying pan over a medium-high heat. Sear the scallops, turning and basting with glaze every 2 minutes, until they are just cooked and the bacon is crisp, 5–7 minutes.

Remove the cocktail sticks and serve the scallops hot with wild rice and the remaining glaze alongside.

BRUSSELS SPROUTS WITH LEMON AND HONEY

This side dish goes well with any kind of meat, but is especially nice with holiday dishes like roast turkey or prime rib. Look for fresh Brussels sprouts still on the stalk; you will find them to be less bitter than loose sprouts.

Serves 4

450g Brussels sprouts, trimmed
4 rashers of thick-cut bacon, coarsely chopped
½ a red onion, thinly sliced
1 tablespoon olive oil
70g honey
1 tablespoon grated lemon zest
Salt
Freshly ground black pepper

Bring a large saucepan of salted water to the boil. Set up an ice bath alongside.

Boil the Brussels sprouts until they are almost tender, about 5 minutes. Drain the sprouts and then immediately plunge them in the ice bath to stop the cooking. Drain well. Pat dry, and cut each sprout in half lengthways.

Cook the bacon in a large frying pan over a medium heat until just starting to crisp, about 6 minutes. Add the onions and continue to cook until the bacon is crisp and the onions are tender, about 2 minutes longer. Transfer to a bowl and cover with foil to keep warm.

Add the olive oil to the same pan the bacon and onions were cooked in and turn the heat up to medium-high. Add the Brussels sprouts and cook until the sprouts are seared brown on the edges, 4–5 minutes. Return the bacon and onions to the pan with the Brussels sprouts. Add the honey and lemon zest. Turn off the heat and stir until the honey is melted and the sprouts are evenly glazed, about 1 minute. Season to taste with salt and pepper.

Serve immediately.

PASTA ALLA CARBONARA

This is a great 'go-to' dish when unexpected guests stop by because so many of the ingredients are usually on hand. Fresh pasta is always best, but if dried pasta is the only option, it works too. More wine, anyone?

Serves 4

1 tablespoon olive oil
4 rashers of bacon, diced
80g grated Parmigiano-Reggiano,
  plus extra to serve
2 large eggs
2 large egg yolks
120ml double cream
½ teaspoon salt
½ teaspoon freshly ground
  black pepper
285g fresh linguine
125g frozen peas, thawed

Bring a large saucepan of salted water to the boil.

Heat the oil in a large frying pan over a medium heat. Add the bacon and cook until it is almost crisp, about 6 minutes. Reduce the heat to low and stir now and then while you prepare the remaining ingredients.

In a medium bowl, whisk together the cheese, eggs, egg yolks, cream, salt and pepper.

Cook the pasta until al dente, following the instructions on the packet. When there is 1 minute remaining on the pasta, add the peas. Drain the pasta and peas, reserving a ladleful of the pasta cooking water. Add the pasta, peas and reserved liquid to the pan with the bacon. Toss gently to combine. Add the cheese and egg mixture and toss gently. Cook until the pasta is warm and thoroughly coated in the sauce, about 2 minutes.

Serve immediately with additional Parmigiano-Reggiano cheese and black pepper alongside.

FAVOURITE FRENCH LENTILS

Lentils may not be the first thing that comes to mind when the cuisine of France is discussed, but the French do prepare them brilliantly. French green lentils, also known as Puy lentils, are more plump and meaty than the common brown or orange varieties. This hearty warm dish is also delicious served cold as a salad the next day. Peeling pearl onions can be labour intensive so you can do them one day ahead and store in the fridge.

Serves 4

175g white pearl onions (about 15 onions)
6 rashers of bacon, coarsely chopped
1 large carrot, sliced
4 garlic cloves, thinly sliced
2 teaspoons salt
½ teaspoon freshly ground black pepper
170g French green lentils, rinsed
1 litre water
5 fresh thyme sprigs
1 bay leaf
3 tablespoons unsalted butter
1 tablespoon Dijon mustard
Fresh crusty bread or toasted baguette slices

To peel the pearl onions, bring a saucepan of water to the boil and arrange an ice bath alongside. Blanch the onions in the water for 1 minute. Scoop the onions out of the water and plunge them into the waiting ice bath to stop the cooking. Drain the onions and use your fingers to pop the onions from their loosened skins.

Cook the bacon in a large frying pan over a medium heat until almost crisp, about 5 minutes. Add the peeled onions and cook for 5 minutes more. Add the carrots, garlic, salt and pepper and cook until the vegetables are soft and the onions are slightly caramelized, about 5 minutes. Stir in the lentils, water, thyme sprigs and bay leaf. Bring the lentils to the boil and then reduce the heat to low and simmer, uncovered, until the lentils are tender and most of the liquid has been absorbed, 20–30 minutes.

Add the butter and mustard just before serving. Stir until the butter is melted and the ingredients are evenly combined.

Serve warm with bread or toasted baguette slices.

KOREAN-STYLE HANGOVER STEW

This spicy stew is treasured as a remedy for the previous night's excesses. Kimchi is the answer for pretty much all that ails you, according to many Korean grandmothers. This spicy, hearty stew will get you back on your feet in no time. Cabbage kimchi, firm tofu and mirin are widely available. You may have to go to a Korean market for kochujang, a marvellous fermented chilli paste. There is no real substitute, so it is worth seeking out. Kochukaru is a fine red chilli powder that is flavourful without being too fiery. If your head is pounding so hard you can't leave the house, you can use other chilli pastes and unseasoned chilli powders. You will need to adjust the quantity.

Heat the sesame oil in a large saucepan over a medium heat. Add the bacon and onion and cook until the onions are softened and the bacon is browned but not crisp, about 5 minutes. Stir in the garlic and ginger and cook for 1 minute more. Add the chilli paste and chilli powder and stir to combine. Add the chopped kimchi with juices and the water.

Bring the soup to the boil and then reduce the heat to low. Add the tofu and simmer gently for 20–30 minutes to deepen the flavours. Season with mirin and soy sauce.

Top with spring onions and serve hot with white rice.

Serves 4

1 tablespoon sesame oil
6 rashers of thick-cut bacon,
  cut into 5cm pieces
1 onion, thinly sliced
2 garlic cloves, crushed
1 tablespoon grated fresh ginger
1 tablespoon kochujang (Korean
  fermented red chilli paste)
1 tablespoon kochukaru (fine
  Korean red chilli powder)
200g kimchi with juices, chopped
1 litre water
400g firm tofu, drained and cubed
60ml mirin
1 tablespoon soy sauce
70g spring onions, sliced
  (about 1 bunch)
350g cooked white rice

CRAB AND CORN CHOWDER

Rich, complex and easy to make for a weeknight supper. If you can't find fresh Dungeness crab meat, you may substitute a variety that is fresh in your area.

Serves 4–6

6 rashers of thick-cut bacon, coarsely chopped
1 onion, chopped
2 celery sticks, chopped
2 medium carrots, chopped
1 teaspoon salt
½ teaspoon freshly ground black pepper
1 red pepper, chopped
2 garlic cloves, crushed
2 teaspoons dried thyme
2 tablespoons plain flour
120ml dry white wine
1 litre chicken or fish stock
1 bay leaf
225g baby red potatoes or new potatoes, quartered
450g Dungeness crab meat, picked clean of any shells
280g fresh or frozen sweetcorn
120ml double cream
2 teaspoons chopped fresh parsley
¼ teaspoon cayenne pepper
Fresh, crusty bread or bite-sized crackers

Cook the bacon in a large saucepan over a medium heat until crisp, about 8 minutes. Transfer to kitchen paper, reserving the rendered bacon fat in the pan.

Cook the onion, celery, carrot, salt and black pepper in the bacon fat until the onions are soft and translucent, about 5 minutes. Add the red pepper, garlic and thyme and cook for another 2 minutes. Stir in the flour, making sure that the vegetables are evenly coated. Add the wine and leave it to simmer and reduce slightly. Add the stock, bay leaf and the potatoes. Bring the soup to the boil over a high heat, reduce the temperature to medium-low and simmer uncovered, for about 20 minutes. Add the crab and corn and simmer gently until the potatoes and corn are tender, about 5 additional minutes.

Finish with the cream and keep warm until ready to serve.

Just before serving, stir in the parsley and cayenne pepper. Ladle the soup into bowls and top with the reserved crumbled bacon. Serve bowls of soup with crusty bread or crackers.

BACON-WRAPPED BEEF TENDERLOINS WITH POMEGRANATE GLAZE

As with bacon, if you are going to indulge in something, it only makes sense to buy the very best. Go to your local butcher and buy steaks that will make you proud. You might want to make a little extra sauce to keep your guests from licking their plates at such a nice dinner.

Serves 4

4 beef tenderloin steaks
  (125–175g each)
Salt
Coarsely ground black pepper
4 rashers of thick-cut, peppered
  bacon
2 tablespoons olive oil
Pomegranate Glaze
  (recipe opposite)

Preheat the oven to 230°C (Gas 8).

Sprinkle each steak very generously with salt and pepper. Wrap each steak with one rasher of bacon, securing the ends with a cocktail stick.

Heat the olive oil in a large ovenproof frying pan, preferably cast-iron, over a high heat. Sear the steaks to a nice brown, about 2 minutes on each side. Using a pair of tongs, carefully roll the steaks on their sides to sear the bacon all the way around. Transfer the pan to the oven and cook, flipping the steaks once halfway through cooking, until the steaks are done to your liking and the bacon is just cooked through, about 5–7 minutes for medium-rare. Remove and discard the cocktail sticks.

Serve the steaks hot, drizzled with Pomegranate Glaze.

POMEGRANATE GLAZE

240ml pomegranate juice
120ml balsamic vinegar
60ml light brown sugar
4 teaspoons chopped
  fresh rosemary
Salt

Combine the pomegranate juice, vinegar, sugar and rosemary in a saucepan. Bring to the boil over a high heat, then simmer over a medium heat until reduced by half, about 15–18 minutes. Season to taste with salt.

*Over the top bacon lover's tip:

Brush the steaks with a little melted Clarified Bacon Fat (page 20) before seasoning.

CHICKEN NORMANDY, OF SORTS

Normandy is famed for their apple orchards. Consider this variation of a classic recipe next time you feel yourself trapped in a chicken breast rut. It's quick to prepare and especially warming on a chilly autumn evening when served with mashed potatoes.

Serves 4

4 rashers of bacon, coarsely
   chopped
4 skin-on, boneless chicken breasts
Salt
Freshly ground black pepper
35g plain flour
½ a small onion, thinly sliced
120ml dry sherry
240ml apple cider
1 crisp red apple, sliced
1 tablespoon chopped fresh thyme
120ml double cream

Cook the bacon in a large frying pan over a medium heat until crisp, about 8 minutes. Transfer to kitchen paper, reserving the rendered bacon fat in the pan. Season the chicken on all sides with salt and pepper. Dredge the chicken with flour, shaking to remove the excess. Cook the chicken in the reserved bacon fat over a medium heat until it is golden brown and nearly cooked through, about 6 minutes per side. Remove the chicken from the pan and keep it warm while you prepare the sauce.

Cook the onions in the pan until they are soft and translucent, about 6 minutes. Add the sherry and simmer to reduce it slightly. Add the cider and simmer until reduced by half, about 5 minutes. Add the apples, thyme and cooked bacon to the sauce and stir to combine. Stir in the cream and add the chicken breasts with any juices that may have collected in the pan. Simmer until the chicken is fully cooked, about 5 additional minutes. Serve hot.

WRAPPED-UP, GLAZED-UP PORK TENDERLOIN

Without question, this is one of the most popular recipes in the whole book. The pork is juicy, tender and flavourful and the easy-to-make glaze tastes like it took all day to make. This recipe makes extra rub for another use.

Serves 4

1 (450g) pork tenderloin
2 tablespoons light brown sugar
1 tablespoon paprika
1 tablespoon freshly ground
  black pepper
1 tablespoon coarse salt
2 teaspoons chilli powder
¼ teaspoon cayenne pepper
6 rashers of thin-cut, applewood
  smoked bacon
2 tablespoons olive oil
375g good-quality apricot jam
125g sweet-hot mustard
1 tablespoon chopped fresh
  rosemary

Preheat the oven to 180°C (Gas 4). Trim the pork of excess fat and membrane.

In a small bowl, combine the brown sugar, paprika, black pepper, salt, chilli powder and cayenne. Rub the pork generously with the spice mixture. Store any extra spice rub in an airtight container for another use.

Wrap the pork in rashers of bacon, overlapping the pieces slightly and tucking the ends underneath to hold them in place.

Heat the oil in a roasting pan or a large ovenproof frying pan over a medium-high heat. Sear the pork until it is brown on all sides, about 8 minutes total. Transfer the pan to the oven and bake the tenderloin until the core temperature reaches 68°C, about 15 minutes.

While the pork is cooking, whisk together the apricot jam and the mustard in a small saucepan. Warm the mixture over a medium-low heat until it begins to bubble, about 5 minutes. Remove the pan from the heat and stir in the rosemary. A few minutes before the pork is ready to come out of the oven, spoon a few tablespoons of glaze evenly over the meat. Continue cooking just to set the glaze.

Serve hot slices of the pork with the remaining glaze alongside.

ONION AND
BACON JAM

In Seattle, the buzz about Bacon Jam started when a local food truck, Skillet, started slathering it on their fabulous burgers and hot sandwiches. Jars of Skillet's Original Bacon Jam are now available online, but inspired chefs may prefer to make their own version. This is our favourite, with roasted garlic and shallots and a hint of black coffee. Use a spoonful with eggs, slather it on a cheese toastie or put a delicate dollop on a canapé. The possibilities are endless.

Makes about 720g

5 garlic cloves, unpeeled
2 shallots, unpeeled
2 tablespoons extra-virgin olive oil
450g bacon, coarsely chopped
450g red onions, sliced
3 tablespoons light brown sugar
3 tablespoons maple syrup
1 teaspoon paprika
1 teaspoon ground cumin
1 teaspoon ground coriander
240ml coffee
60ml sherry vinegar
1 teaspoon salt
1 teaspoon freshly ground
   black pepper

Preheat the oven to 200°C
(Gas 6).

Cut the garlic cloves and shallots in half, exposing the flesh but leaving the skins on. Place them on a double piece of foil and drizzle with the olive oil, tossing to coat. Seal the foil into a pouch and bake until the garlic and shallots are soft,

about 30 minutes. Cool slightly until easy to handle, and remove the skins.

While the garlic and onions are roasting, cook the bacon in a large casserole or saucepan over a medium heat until crisp, working in batches if needed, about 8 minutes per batch. Transfer to kitchen paper, reserving the rendered bacon fat in the pan.

Pour out all but 60ml of the bacon fat. Save any extra fat for Clarified Bacon Fat (page 20). Add the sliced onions and cook, stirring occasionally, until the onions are soft, 10–12 minutes. Add the roasted garlic and shallots, mashing them a bit with the back of a spoon.

Return the bacon to the pan and stir in the remaining ingredients. Reduce the heat to low and simmer, partially covered, until the mixture becomes a deep, rich colour and jam-like texture, about 2 hours. If the mixture begins to dry out before it is dark and soft, add a few tablespoons of water and stir often to prevent the jam from burning.

Transfer the jam to the bowl of a food processor and pulse until the jam is roughly chopped and more spreadable.

Serve warm or store refrigerated in an airtight container for up to 2 weeks.

BUCATINI ALL'AMATRICIANA

Bucatini is a long pasta with a very thin hole in the centre, so it is kind of like chewy spaghetti tubes. Sauce amatriciana is one of the oldest Italian tomato sauces. It is traditionally made with guanciale, or smoked pork cheek, but bacon has become a more common ingredient. Serve the pasta with plenty of grated Pecorino-Romano cheese, a loaf of crusty bread and a good bottle of red wine.

Serves 4

1 tablespoon extra-virgin olive oil
4 rashers of thick-cut bacon, coarsely chopped
1 small onion, finely chopped
3 garlic cloves, sliced
60ml white wine
2 (400g) tins of whole tomatoes with juices
2 tablespoons balsamic vinegar
½ teaspoon dried chilli flakes
½ teaspoon salt
¼ teaspoon freshly ground black pepper
450g bucatini pasta, or substitute spaghetti
25g grated Pecorino-Romano cheese, plus extra to serve

Heat the oil in a large frying pan over a medium heat. Add the bacon and cook until it is just beginning to crisp, about 6 minutes. Add the onion and garlic, and cook until the onion is transparent, about 3 minutes. Add the wine and simmer to reduce, about 2 minutes longer. Add the tomatoes and vinegar. Crush the tomatoes with a spoon as they soften. Simmer until the sauce comes together, about 10 minutes. Season with chilli flakes, salt and pepper. Keep the sauce warm over a low heat while you cook the pasta.

Bring a large saucepan of salted water to the boil. Cook the pasta until al dente, following the packet instructions. Drain well, reserving a ladleful of pasta cooking water. Add the pasta and reserved liquid to the sauce and return the pan to a medium heat. Toss the pasta gently until it is well coated and heated through, about 5 minutes. Fold in the Pecorino cheese.

Serve the pasta hot with additional cheese alongside.

DARK

DARK

BACON MANHATTAN

Bacon-infused bourbon adds a gentle, savoury perfume to this classic cocktail.

Makes 1 cocktail

2–3 dashes bitters
40ml Bacon-infused Bourbon
  (recipe opposite)
15ml dry vermouth
7ml sweet vermouth
1 maraschino cherry or
  1 brandied cherry
1 twist of orange rind
1 strip of crisp, cooked bacon
  or Candied Bacon (page 154),
  to garnish

Swirl 2–3 dashes of bitters in a chilled martini glass. Fill a cocktail shaker with large ice cubes and add the bourbon and vermouths. Shake vigorously. Strain the cocktail into the prepared martini glass and garnish with the cherry, orange rind and bacon. Serve immediately.

BACON-INFUSED BOURBON

This technique can be used to add a scent of bacon to many different liquids.

Makes 340ml of infused bourbon

340ml bourbon
55g Clarified Bacon Fat (page 20),
  melted

Combine the bourbon and bacon fat in a large jar. Seal with a tightly fitting lid and shake vigorously. Leave the bourbon to infuse at room temperature for 5–8 hours. Put the jar in the freezer and freeze until all of the bacon fat has solidified at the surface of the bourbon, about 1 hour. Scoop off and discard the bacon fat and strain the bourbon through a fine-mesh sieve lined with 2 coffee filters. Store the bacon-infused bourbon at room temperature for up to 2 weeks, or in the fridge for up to 6 months.

CLAMS CASINO

No good cocktail or patio party of the 1950s would have been complete without a piping hot tray of Clams Casino. We think it is a tradition that should be revived, and improved upon. Use only fresh, live clams.

Makes 24 clams

Rock salt or kosher salt,
  as needed for baking
24 hard-shell clams,
  scrubbed clean
2 tablespoons olive oil
3 rashers of bacon, finely chopped
1 red pepper, deseeded and finely
  chopped
1 large shallot, finely chopped
2 garlic cloves, crushed
½ teaspoon dried oregano
60ml dry white wine
Grated zest and juice of 1 lemon
20g Parmesan cheese, grated
Salt
Freshly ground black pepper

Cover a baking tray with a thick, even layer of rock or kosher salt.

Shuck the clams, wearing a shucking glove for safety. Hold a clam securely while you insert a shucking knife between the shells. Pry the shells apart and sever the adductor muscle connecting the shells. Discard the top shell. Loosen the clam meat and the muscle in the lower shell. Nestle the shucked clams in the prepared salt tray. Cover and refrigerate the clams while you prepare the remaining ingredients.

Heat the oil in a large frying pan over a medium heat. Cook the bacon until it is crisp, about 8 minutes. Transfer to kitchen paper, reserving the rendered bacon fat in the pan. Cook the red pepper, shallot, garlic and oregano in the remaining bacon fat until the shallots are tender and translucent, about 5 minutes. Add the wine and the lemon juice and simmer until the liquid has almost completely evaporated. Transfer the mixture to a bowl and cool slightly.

Stir the reserved bacon, 2 tablespoons of the Parmesan cheese and the lemon zest into the cooled vegetable mixture. Season with salt and pepper to taste.

Preheat the oven to 260°C (Gas 10).

Spoon 1–2 teaspoons of the bacon and vegetable mixture onto each clam, mounding the topping slightly. Sprinkle with the remaining Parmesan cheese. Bake until the clams are cooked through and the topping is golden, about 10 minutes.

Serve immediately.

BACON-WRAPPED STUFFED DATES

We all could use a really hot date now and then, right? Make these ahead of time and pop them in the oven when your guests arrive. Medjool dates are particularly large, moist and meaty. The vinegar and orange juice adds a tangy balance to the sweet and salty flavours.

Makes 20 dates

20 pitted Medjool dates
55g blue cheese, crumbled
10 rashers of bacon, cut in half
  crossways, par-cooked (page 12)
120ml balsamic vinegar
Grated zest and juice of 1 orange

Preheat the oven to 230°C (Gas 8). Line a baking tray with baking parchment.

With a paring knife, make a slit in the centre of each date. Carefully stuff each date with 1 teaspoon of the crumbled blue cheese and wrap with bacon, securing the ends with a cocktail stick. Place the wrapped dates on the prepared tray and bake for 5 minutes. Flip the dates and bake for an additional 5 minutes, or until the bacon is crisp and the blue cheese begins to ooze.

While the dates are baking, combine the vinegar, orange zest and orange juice in a small saucepan. Bring the mixture to the boil over a high heat and then reduce the heat to medium-high and simmer until the mixture has reduced to a thick, syrupy glaze, about 10 minutes. Strain the glaze through a fine-mesh sieve.

Remove the cocktail sticks from the dates, arrange them on a serving platter and drizzle with the glaze.

Serve warm.

BAKED POTATO SKINS

For best results, bake the potatoes in the oven. If you cheat and use the microwave, the skins don't seem to come out as crisp. Serve these as a side dish to grilled steak or barbecued chicken.

Makes 8

4 baking potatoes
500g soured cream
2–3 tablespoons ranch salad
   dressing mix
6 rashers of bacon, cooked and
   crumbled
115g Cheddar cheese, grated
2 tablespoons thinly sliced
   fresh chives

Preheat the oven to 230°C (Gas 8). Wash and dry the potatoes, and pierce the skins all over with a fork. Bake the potatoes directly on the oven rack until they are tender and the skins are crisp, about 1 hour.

In a medium bowl, whisk together the soured cream, ranch salad dressing mix, crumbled bacon and three-quarters of the cheese.

Remove the cooked potatoes from the oven and reduce the oven temperature to 180°C (Gas 4). While the potatoes are still hot, cut them in half and scoop out the flesh, leaving the skins intact. We like to cut them crossways so they form nice serving cups. Add the hot potato flesh to the soured cream mixture and blend with a potato masher or electric mixer until evenly combined.

Spoon the soured cream and potato mixture back into the skins and arrange the potato halves on a baking tray. Sprinkle the tops with the remaining cheese.

Bake the skins until the cheese is melted and the potatoes are heated through, about 30 minutes.

Garnish with chives and serve hot.

*Over the top bacon lover's tip:

Before putting the potatoes in the oven, rub the skins with a little Clarified Bacon Fat (page 20).

BACON CHEESE PUFFS

These buttery, airy spheres of perfection will go so fast you will have to fight to sample the fruits of your labour. They are super simple to make and many of the ingredients are common staples, so you may find yourself making them quite often. Comté cheese is a rich, nutty cave-aged French cheese. You can also substitute Parmesan or mature Cheddar.

Makes about 24 cheese puffs

120ml water
55g unsalted butter, cubed
¼ teaspoon salt
35g plain flour
2 large eggs
75g Comté cheese, grated
4 rashers of cooked and crumbled, peppered bacon
2 teaspoons chopped fresh herbs, such as chives, thyme and/or marjoram

Preheat the oven to 220°C (Gas 7). Line a baking tray with baking parchment.

In a medium saucepan, combine the water, butter and salt. Heat the pan over a medium heat until the butter is melted and the water just begins to boil. Add the flour all at once and stir vigorously with a wooden spoon until the dough comes together in a ball that pulls away from the sides of the pan, about 3 minutes. Test the dough by giving the pan a few good shakes. If the ball stays together, it is done.

Transfer the dough to the bowl of an electric mixer. Cool for 5 minutes. Beat the dough at a low speed with the paddle attachment, while adding the eggs, one at a time. Make sure the first egg is fully incorporated before adding the second. The finished dough should be smooth and shiny. Stir in two-thirds of the grated cheese, the bacon and herbs.

Transfer the dough to a piping bag fitted with a 15mm wide, plain nozzle. Pipe the dough onto the parchment-lined baking tray in 2.5cm mounds spaced about 5cm apart. Use the back of a spoon dipped in water to pat down any pointed tips. Sprinkle with the remaining cheese.

Bake for 10 minutes, then reduce the oven temperature to 190°C (Gas 5) and bake for an additional 20–25 minutes, or until the cheese puffs are a deep, golden brown colour. Serve warm.

*Over the top bacon lover's tip:

Brush mounds of dough with a little melted Clarified Bacon Fat (page 20) before sprinkling with the remaining cheese and baking.

Candied Bacon

CANDIED BACON S'MORES

This little gem may have your friends around the campfire gasping with delight. Candied bacon is light and sturdy enough to pack into even remote locations. Bacon laced bars of dark chocolate are available at many gourmet shops. If camping isn't your thing, these can also be made at home by toasting the marshmallows over a direct flame and warming the assembled S'mores to drippy perfection in the oven.

Makes 4

4 jumbo marshmallows
4 (5cm) pieces of Candied Bacon (recipe opposite)
4 (5cm) squares of dark chocolate
4 digestive biscuits, halved

Roast the marshmallows over an open flame until golden brown, puffed and gooey on the inside. Sandwich the warm marshmallows with the candied bacon and chocolate between layers of biscuit.

Serve immediately.

CANDIED BACON

Makes 12 slices

100g granulated sugar
100g light brown sugar
1 tablespoon ground cinnamon
12 rashers of thick-cut bacon

Preheat the oven to 190°C (Gas 5). Arrange a wire rack over a foil-lined baking tray.

In a medium bowl, combine the sugar, brown sugar and ground cinnamon. Add the bacon rashers and toss to coat.

Lay the sugar-coated bacon rashers on wire rack and bake, flipping once, until the bacon is crisp and the sugar is caramelized, 25–30 minutes. Cool slightly on the rack before removing.

Serve immediately or store in an airtight container in the fridge for up to 1 week.

CARDAMOM CUPCAKES WITH MAPLE, BACON AND CREAM CHEESE FROSTING

These cupcakes have a lovely balance of spice and sweetness. But let's face it, it's the frosting that really counts when it comes to cupcakes. Our Maple, Bacon and Cream Cheese version is a showstopper on virtually any cupcake flavour, including classic vanilla, carrot cake or chocolate.

Makes 12 cupcakes

175g plain flour
1¼ teaspoons baking powder
1 teaspoon ground cardamom
½ teaspoon ground ginger
¼ teaspoon grated nutmeg
¼ teaspoon salt
⅛ teaspoon ground cloves
115g unsalted butter, softened
65g granulated sugar
65g dark brown sugar
2 large eggs
½ teaspoon vanilla extract
120ml buttermilk
Maple, Bacon and Cream Cheese
  Frosting (page 159)
Candied Bacon (page 154), cut into
  small pieces, to decorate

Preheat the oven to 180°C (Gas 4). Fill a 12-cup cupcake tin with paper liners.

Sift together the flour, baking powder, cardamom, ginger, nutmeg, salt and cloves. Sift onto a large sheet of non-stick baking parchment to make pouring it into the mixing bowl more convenient.

In the bowl of an electric mixer, whip the butter and sugars together until light and fluffy, about 3 minutes on a medium-high speed. Add the eggs one at a time, waiting until each egg is fully incorporated before adding the next and scraping down the sides of the bowl after each addition. Add the vanilla. Reduce the mixer speed slightly and alternate adding the dry ingredients and the buttermilk, beginning and ending with the dry ingredients.

Divide the batter evenly among the cupcake tin, filling each cup about two-thirds full. Bake the cupcakes until a skewer comes out clean when inserted near the centre, 18–22 minutes. For even cooking, rotate the cupcake tin halfway through the baking time. Cool the cupcakes for 5 minutes in the tin, then transfer them to a rack and cool completely.

Frost with Maple, Bacon and Cream Cheese Frosting and decorate with Candied Bacon.

MAPLE, BACON AND CREAM CHEESE FROSTING

Makes enough to ice 12 cupcakes

225g cream cheese, softened
115g unsalted butter, softened
2 tablespoons pure maple syrup
275g icing sugar, sifted
25g toasted pecans, chopped
3 rashers of cooked and crumbled
   bacon

In an electric mixer, beat the cream cheese and butter on a medium speed until smooth and evenly combined. Add the maple syrup. With the mixer on low, gradually add the icing sugar until the frosting is thick and spreadable. Fold in the toasted pecans and bacon bits.

BACON CASHEW CARAMEL CORN

This is a very special caramel corn, so save it for very special movie nights or events. Or, put it in a decorative container or gift bag and give it as a gift at Christmas. Substitute brandy or Cognac for the apple brandy if it is unavailable. We suggest that you pop the corn in a hot-air style popper, or microwave the kernels in plain brown lunch bags for about 3 minutes on high. Work in batches, using only 2 tablespoons of popcorn kernels per bag.

Makes about 100g

85g popped corn (made from
   about 100g popcorn kernels)
12 rashers of cooked and crumbled
   bacon
120g roasted, salted cashews
200g sugar
4 tablespoons unsalted butter
60ml water
2 tablespoons golden syrup
60ml double cream
2 tablespoons Calvados
   (apple brandy)
1 teaspoon fleur de sel

Preheat the oven to 150°C
(Gas 2).

In a very large bowl, toss together the popped corn, bacon bits and cashews.

Line a baking tray with foil and brush evenly with oil.

Stir the sugar, butter, water and golden syrup together in a saucepan. Cook over a medium heat, stirring until the sugar dissolves and the butter is melted.

Increase the temperature to medium-high and boil, without stirring, until the syrup turns a deep amber colour, about 13 minutes. While the syrup cooks, you may want to carefully swirl the pan and brush down the sides carefully with a wet pastry brush to prevent any sugar crystals from forming, but do not stir.

Remove the syrup from the heat and immediately pour in the cream. Protect your face and hands, as there will be a lot of steam and the syrup will bubble violently. Add the Calvados and stir until well blended. Immediately pour the hot caramel mixture over the popcorn mixture and toss with a large spoon or spatula coated with oil until evenly mixed. Transfer the mixture to the oiled tray.

Bake the corn for 20 minutes, tossing every few minutes for even crispness. Sprinkle with fleur de sel. Cool completely and transfer to an airtight container until ready to serve.

*Over the top bacon lover's tip:

Pop popcorn in Clarified Bacon Fat (page 20) on the hob.

BACON BAKLAVA

How can those delicate layers of pastry and nuts possibly be improved upon, except with bacon? Filo pastry can seem scary to make at first, but once you understand that the sheer quantity of layers will mask the flaws of any individual sheet, you will gain confidence. Orange flower water and rose water are available at good supermarkets, gourmet shops and online.

Makes about 24 servings

225g raw walnut pieces
225g raw pistachio nuts, shelled
12 rashers of cooked and crumbled
    bacon
65g sugar
1 teaspoon ground cardamom
285g unsalted butter, melted
450g shop-bought filo pastry
240ml water
200g sugar
280g honey
1 cinnamon stick
60ml orange flower water
    or rose water

Preheat the oven to 180°C (Gas 4).

In a food processor, pulse the nuts until they are ground. Add the bacon, sugar and cardamom and pulse a few more times until the nut mixture is finely chopped and evenly blended.

Begin layering the baklava. Brush a Swiss roll tin or baking tray with sides, generously with the melted butter. Unroll the filo pastry and cover the sheets with a piece of cling film and a clean, damp tea towel. This keeps the sheets from drying out while you are layering the baklava. Read the packet for detailed handling instructions.

Place a sheet of filo in the tin and brush it with melted butter. Repeat with 6 more sheets of filo pastry and butter for a total of 7 sheets. You do not have to cover every last inch of the filo with butter, but try and have it evenly dispersed between all of the layers. Spread about 50g of the nut mixture evenly over the filo. Top the nuts with two more buttered sheets of filo. Continue sprinkling with another 50g of the nut mixture adding two sheets of buttered filo until all of the nut mixture is used. Top with a final layer of 7 buttered filo sheets.

Use a sharp knife to cut the uncooked baklava into 24 diamond shapes. Bake the baklava until it is brown and crisp, 30–35 minutes.

While the baklava is baking, combine the water, sugar and honey in a saucepan. Gradually heat the mixture until the sugar dissolves. Add the cinnamon stick and bring the mixture to the boil. Reduce the heat slightly and simmer for 25–30 minutes. Remove the pan from the heat, add the orange flower water and cool slightly. Pour the syrup evenly over the baklava as soon as it comes out of the oven. Make sure you get the syrup in every crack and crevice. Leave to soak for several hours. Serve at room temperature and store leftovers in the fridge.

BACON, PEANUT BUTTER AND CHOCOLATE CHIP COOKIES

Bacon, peanut butter and chocolate, it's like a trifecta of bliss. This dough freezes well, so there is no reason why you can't have a batch ready to bake off at any time.

Makes about 24 (7.5cm) cookies

170g plain flour
¾ teaspoon bicarbonate of soda
½ teaspoon baking powder
¼ teaspoon salt
115g unsalted butter, softened
100g granulated sugar, plus extra
   for rolling the cookies
100g light brown sugar
115g peanut butter
1 large egg
1 teaspoon vanilla extract
50g roasted, salted peanuts,
   finely chopped
85g chocolate chips
3 rashers of cooked and crumbled
   bacon

Preheat the oven to 180°C (Gas 4). Line 2 baking trays with non-stick baking parchment.

Sift together the flour, bicarbonate of soda, baking powder and salt. Sift it onto a large sheet of baking parchment to make pouring it into the mixing bowl more convenient.

Beat the butter with an electric mixer on a medium-high speed until smooth. Add both sugars and continue to beat until light and fluffy, 3–4 minutes. Beat in the peanut butter until fully incorporated. Beat in the egg and vanilla until thoroughly combined.

Reduce the mixer speed to low and mix in the flour mixture in 2 additions, scraping down the sides of the bowl as needed. Stir in the peanuts, chocolate chips and bacon.

Pour some granulated sugar in a small bowl. Shape the cookie dough into 7.5cm balls. Roll the balls in sugar and place them 5cm apart on the prepared baking trays. Flatten the cookies with the tines of a fork dipped in cold water to form a crisscross pattern.

Bake the cookies until they are golden brown, 12–14 minutes. For best results, rotate the trays front to back and top to bottom halfway through cooking.

Cool the cookies for 2 minutes on the baking trays before transferring them to a rack to cool completely.

BACON BUTTERMILK CARAMELS

Another great gift idea or a special holiday treat, these caramels have a hint of saltiness and a sophisticated flavour that will please young and old alike.

Makes 48 pieces

45g hazelnuts
6 rashers of cooked and crumbled
  bacon
180ml buttermilk
180ml double cream
210g icing sugar
100g light brown sugar
110g golden syrup
55g unsalted butter
¼ teaspoon salt
1 teaspoon vanilla extract

Preheat the oven to 200°C (Gas 6).

Toast the hazelnuts in the oven until the skins are dark and the interiors are lightly browned and fragrant, about 8 minutes. Transfer the nuts to a clean tea towel and rub briskly to remove the skins. Chop coarsely.

Spray an 20cm square baking tin with cooking spray. Cut 2 (20 x 38cm) pieces of non-stick baking parchment and lay one vertically and one horizontally in the tin so the tin is fully lined with extra paper coming up over the sides. This will help you remove the caramels from the tin once they are cool. Spray the parchment with cooking spray. Sprinkle the chopped hazelnuts and bacon evenly on the bottom of the baking tin. Set aside.

Combine the buttermilk and cream in a large measuring jug. Pour half of the mixed buttermilk and cream into a medium saucepan with the icing sugar, brown sugar, golden syrup, butter and salt. Cook over a medium heat, stirring constantly, until the sugar is dissolved. Continue to cook without stirring for about 10 minutes.

Stir in the remaining cream mixture and continue to cook until the temperature reaches 121°C on a sugar thermometer. Remove the pan from the heat and stir in the vanilla, being careful to protect your hands and face from any steam or bubbles. Immediately pour the hot caramel into the prepared tin. Leave to cool completely, at least 1 hour, or overnight.

When the caramel is completely cold, lift it out of the tin with the parchment paper. Cut the caramel into 48 even-sized pieces using a large, lightly oiled knife. Wrap each caramel decoratively with greaseproof paper and string. Store at room temperature for up to 2 weeks.

APPLE PIE WITH BACON STREUSEL

It's almost an American obligation to love apple pie. But we expect apple pie with bacon may become more of a worldwide phenomenon. The apple mixture is boldly spiced to stand up to a streusel topping laced with bacon bits and crystallized ginger. The pastry case is double baked for crispness. Cover the edges with foil if it is getting too dark while baking.

Makes 1 (23cm) pie

2 medium Granny Smith apples, peeled, halved, cored and thinly sliced
2 medium Braeburn apples, peeled, halved, cored and thinly sliced
60ml lemon juice
1 teaspoon apple cider vinegar
½ teaspoon ground cinnamon
½ teaspoon ground allspice
¼ teaspoon grated nutmeg
100g granulated sugar
100g light brown sugar
70g plain flour
1 Tender and Flaky Pastry Case (page 27)
Bacon Streusel (recipe opposite)

Preheat the oven to 190°C (Gas 5).

Toss together the apple slices, lemon juice and vinegar in a large bowl. In a small bowl, combine the cinnamon, allspice, nutmeg, sugars and flour. Toss the apples and spice mixture together to coat.

Fill the pastry case with the apple mixture and top with the Bacon Streusel. Bake until the top is browned and the apples are tender, 50–60 minutes. Serve warm or at room temperature.

BACON STREUSEL:

70g plain flour
100g light brown sugar
115g very cold, unsalted butter
6 rashers of cooked and crumbled bacon
2 tablespoons chopped crystallized ginger

In a medium bowl, combine the flour and brown sugar. Shred the cold butter with a cheese grater into the flour mixture and mix until pea-sized clumps form. Add the crumbled bacon and ginger and stir to mix.

If you are not using immediately, store in the fridge until ready to use.

INDEX

ACKNOWLEDGEMENTS

The creation of this little volume came together because of a team made up of people both inside the Armstrong-Pitts Studios and out.

To start, Theresa Gilliam did an amazing job creating the recipes, along with Jean Galton, who edited her recipes, came up with wonderful tasty ways to eat bacon I'd never thought of. Theresa's food styling made every one of her recipes come to life, looking as good as they tasted.

Thanks to Susan Volland for helping us add a bit of wit to the copy. We're grateful to Christophe Servieres for his diligent assistance in tracking all things technical, and once again being the 'go-to guy' keeping the studio on track and presentable even after several days of bacon grease. The graphic design of this book is the vision of Xiaonan Wang. And we don't know what we'd do without our design mentor Alicia Nammacher, who was there in the trenches with us every step of the way in production and designed the wonderful cover.

A special thanks goes to our ardent supporter and bacon donor, Wilson Winn, who gave us endless supplies of wonderful bacon.

The end thanks goes to the agent for Our Little Book Company – Alison Fargis of Stonesong who kept believing that if she knocked on enough doors to get this published, one would open and eventually it did with the editor of this tome, Ann Treistman from The Countryman Press.

EJ Armstrong

Our Little Book Company
A Black Building Production